ReShaping Faith
21 Day
Devotional Journal

Chaplain Dorcus Cater, MDIV., BCC

Copyright © 2025 by Dorcus Cater

All rights reserved. No part of this publication may be reproduced or transmitted in any form or by any means electronic or mechanical, including photocopying, recording, or any information storage and retrieval system now known or to be invented, whatsoever, without the express written permission of the publisher except for the use of brief quotations for the inclusion in a magazine, newspaper, website, or broadcast.

All Scriptures in this book are Public Domain (American Standard Version (ASV), King James Version (KJV), World English Bible, (WEB) and are taken from www.biblegateway.com.

ReShaping Faith™ is a trademark of Reshaping Faith Publishing, LLC

ISBN: 979-8-9929991-4-3

Published in the United States by
ReShaping Faith Publishing, LLC
4002 Highway 78, Suite 530-213
Snellville, Georgia 30039 USA
www.reshapingfaith.com

Cover design by Dorcus Cater

Date: _____

Chapter 1: Rescue Mission

John 3:16-17 (ASV): For God so loved the world, that he gave his only begotten Son, that whosoever believeth on him should not perish, but have eternal life. 17 For God sent not the Son into the world to judge the world; but that the world should be saved through him.

POW! (Pearls of Wisdom): Good people don't go to heaven; only those who accept Jesus as Savior do.

Share what your faith or spiritual path teaches you about heaven, hell, or the afterlife?

Do you find peace, fear, or uncertainty when you think about the afterlife?

If you were wrong about the afterlife, would you want to know?

Date: _____

Chapter 2: Surprised by Death

Luke 12:20-21 (WEB): "But God said to him, 'You foolish one, tonight your soul is required of you. The things which you have prepared—whose will they be?' 21 So is he who lays up treasure for himself, and is not rich toward God."

POW! (Pearls of Wisdom): Death doesn't always wait for us to plan or to get ready for it.

Share your thoughts on your readiness for what happens after death, if death came for you suddenly.

Is there such a thing as dying "too soon"?

Is it better to die suddenly or with time to prepare?

Date: _____

Chapter 3: Rerouted

Ephesians 4:26-27 (WEB): "Be angry, and don't sin." Don't let the sun go down on your wrath, 27 and don't give place to the devil.

POW! (Pearls of Wisdom): Fix your heart. You can't go to the Father's house angry with Him.

Share a time when you were angry with God?

Did you share your grievances with God directly?

Was the situation actually God's fault?

Are you at peace about the situation?

Date: _____

Chapter 4: Unpopular Pardons

2 Peter 3:9 (WEB): The Lord is not slow concerning his promise, as some count slowness; but he is patient with us, not wishing that anyone should perish, but that all should come to repentance.

POW! (Pearls of Wisdom): All sinners are given the opportunity to repent and to reboot their hearts.

Share a time when you committed an act or offense that you believed was unforgiveable.

Are there sins that Jesus cannot or will not forgive? If so, what are they?

What role does repentance play in receiving Jesus' forgiveness?

Date: _____

Chapter 5: Little God

Matthew 12:36-37 (WEB): I tell you that every idle word that men speak, they will give account of it in the day of judgment. 37 For by your words you will be justified, and by your words you will be condemned."

POW! (Pearls of Wisdom): Your words will testify for or against you on that day.

Share your thoughts regarding there being a day of reckoning or a day in which each person will give an account for the words they spoke.

How can someone recognize idols in their own heart or behavior?

What might you be prioritizing above God in your life?

Date: _____

Chapter 6: Misguided Alliance

Exodus 34:14 (WEB): for you shall worship no other god; for Yahweh, whose name is Jealous, is a jealous God.

POW! (Pearls of Wisdom): God is not willing to be a part of a conglomerate of gods. He insists on being the only One on the throne in the hearts of His people.

Share a time when you knowingly or unknowingly embraced or combined spiritual beliefs to create one that worked better for you as an individual.

Do ancestors have spiritual power or influence over the living?

What's the difference between honoring ancestors and worshiping them?

Date: _____

Chapter 7: Bite of Death

1 John 2:16-17 (WEB): For all that is in the world—the lust of the flesh, the lust of the eyes, and the pride of life—isn't the Father's, but is the world's. 17 The world is passing away with its lusts, but he who does God's will remains forever.

POW! (Pearls of Wisdom): Only Jesus can fill the holes in your soul. Nothing in this world can.

Share the things in this world that you depend on to bring you purposeful fulfillment.

What worldly attachments do you struggle to let go of?

How much does your identity rely on status, image, or possessions?

Date: _____

Chapter 8: Opt-Out

Revelation 3:20 (WEB): Behold, I stand at the door and knock. If anyone hears my voice and opens the door, then I will come in to him and will dine with him, and he with me.

POW! (Pearls of Wisdom): Jesus is desperate for us, so much so, that He died on a cross to save us, but He will not override freewill.

Share a time when you sensed Holy Spirit communicating with you about something major, but you ignored or disregarded Him.

Are you living out your own beliefs—or beliefs you inherited?

Have you ever followed a spiritual path out of fear, pressure, or guilt?

Date: _____

Chapter 9: The Sons and Daughters of Abraham

Psalm 8:4 (WEB): what is man, that you think of him? What is the son of man, that you care for him?

POW! (Pearls of Wisdom): Christians do not own the patent on Jesus' love. Jesus does and He shares it with everyone, indiscriminately and without reservation.

Share a time when you were comforted or helped by a stranger, enemy, or unlikely person.

Do you believe that Jesus is concerned about everything that concerns you regardless of your religious beliefs?

Why or why not?

Date: _____

Chapter 10: The Doctor

Ephesians 6:12 (ASV): For our wrestling is not against flesh and blood, but against the principalities, against the powers, against the world-rulers of this darkness, against the spiritual hosts of wickedness in the heavenly places.

POW! (Pearls of Wisdom): The devil does not stand down when you or your loved-one is seeking to be reconciled with Jesus. He ramps up his efforts, but so must you, but in the authority of Jesus' name.

Share a time when you felt an invisible or unknown force working against your efforts to help someone in spiritual trouble.

Are you spiritually awake to the presence of evil in your life and the world?

How do you engage spiritual warfare?

Date: _____

Chapter 11: The Engineer

James 4:7 (WEB): Be subject therefore to God. Resist the devil, and he will flee from you.

POW! (Pearls of Wisdom): Resistance is a weapon of warfare against the devil.

Share a time when you resisted the temptation to react negatively in a challenging situation.

What do you believe made the difference in your ability to resist?

How important are spiritual disciplines in relationship to having the desire and power to resist sin?

Date:

Chapter 12: The Congressman

Proverbs 11:30b (WEB): He who is wise wins souls.

POW! (Pearls of Wisdom): Your kindness is the introduction to your God.

Share a time when your kindness opened a door to an unforeseen spiritual blessing for someone else.

What does it mean to live in alignment with Jesus' love and truth?

~~Is it possible to be both faithful to Scripture and affirming of LGBTQ+ individuals?~~

Date: _____

Chapter 13: Wicked Witnesses

Matthew 19:29 (WEB): Everyone who has left houses, or brothers, or sisters, or father, or mother, or wife, or children, or lands, for my name's sake, will receive one hundred times, and will inherit eternal life.

POW! (Pearls of Wisdom): True Christianity might cost you your families, friends, and more.

Share a time when your commitment to Jesus negatively impacted your relationships.

Are antichrist qualities always overt, or can they be subtle and seductive?

What does it mean for someone to "deny Christ" spiritually or practically?

Date: _____

Chapter 14: Service Connection

Matthew 16:24 (WEB): Then Jesus said to his disciples, "If anyone desires to come after me, let him deny himself, take up his cross, and follow me.

POW! (Pearls of Wisdom): Salvation is free but walking it out will cost you.

Share a time when you lost financially because you opted to do the right thing, in Jesus' name.

Are there areas of your life where you've separated faith from actions?

Are you being honest with yourself about your commitment to your spiritual path?

Date: _____

Chapter 15: Identity Crisis

Isaiah 8:19 (WEB): When they tell you, "Consult with those who have familiar spirits and with the wizards, who chirp and who mutter," shouldn't a people consult with their God? Should they consult the dead on behalf of the living?

POW! (Pearls of Wisdom): Have nothing to do with the dark arts and false religions nor join in with those who practice them. You are inviting demons into your home; your bodily home and where your children sleep.

Share a time when you unknowingly or knowingly dabbled in the dark arts or a false religion.

How do you respond when something in your religion doesn't align with your conscience?

How often do you study sacred texts personally vs. relying on others' interpretations?

Date: _____

Chapter 16: Questionable Companionship

Acts 5:1-10 (Amplified): But a certain man named Ananias, with Sapphira his wife, sold a possession, 2 and kept back part of the price, his wife also being aware of it, then brought a certain part and laid it at the apostles' feet. 3 But Peter said, "Ananias, why has Satan filled your heart to lie to the Holy Spirit and to keep back part of the price of the land? 4 While you kept it, didn't it remain your own? After it was sold, wasn't it in your power? How is it that you have conceived this thing in your heart? You haven't lied to men, but to God." 5 Ananias, hearing these words, fell down and died. Great fear came on all who heard these things. 6 The young men arose and wrapped him up, and they carried him out and buried him. 7 About three hours later, his wife, not knowing what had happened, came in. 8 Peter answered her, "Tell me whether you sold the land for so much." She said, "Yes, for so much." 9 But Peter asked her, "How is it that you have agreed together to tempt the Spirit of the Lord? Behold, the feet of those who have buried your husband are at the door, and they will carry you out." 10 She fell down immediately at his feet and died. The young men came in and found her dead, and they carried her out and buried her by her husband.

POW! (Pearls of Wisdom): Each person is responsible for their own relationship with Jesus. Your spouse can't present you before the Father without spot or wrinkle; only Jesus can.

Share a time when you knowingly or unknowingly placed your relationship with your spouse above God in your heart?

Do you find your worth and identity more in your role as a husband/wife than as a child of God?

Is your spiritual growth dependent on my spouse's faith journey?

Date: _____

Chapter 17: Scorned Woman

Philippians 1:6 (WEB): being confident of this very thing, that he who began a good work in you will complete it until the day of Jesus Christ.

POW! (Pearls of Wisdom): If a person is still breathing without artificial mechanisms, they are still alive. Holy Spirit is still working, therefore, so should you.

Share a time when you gave up on someone or something and they or it wasn't dead.

Do you believe that Jesus is aware of your pain, in real time, and cares deeply about you as you go through it?

What emotions keep surfacing when you think about what happened—anger, grief, fear, betrayal?

Date: _____

Chapter 18: Grief Growl

1 Peter 5:6-7 (WEB): Humble yourselves therefore under the mighty hand of God, that he may exalt you in due time, 7 casting all your worries on him, because he cares for you.

POW! (Pearls of Wisdom): Jesus understands our disappointments. Talk to Him. You don't need words.

Share a time that you trusted God with your raw or angry emotions.

What parts of you are being reshaped by this loss?

What part of you is still holding on, and what part is ready to let go?

Date: _____

Chapter 19: Sound of Despair

Matthew 11:28 (WEB): "Come to me, all you who labor and are heavily burdened, and I will give you rest.

POW! (Pearls of Wisdom): Your depression might also be a "spirit" of heaviness. Command it to go from you, in the name of Jesus and see if your medication works better.

Share a time when you may have knowingly or unknowingly hosted a spirit of heaviness.

Is this despair rooted in unmet expectations, trauma, or a sense of hopelessness?

Can you allow yourself to be held—by God, by others, by grace?

Date: _____

Chapter 20: Faulty Faith

Romans 8:28 (WEB): We know that all things work together for good for those who love God, for those who are called according to his purpose.

POW! (Pearls of Wisdom): A recipe for success in getting your prayers answered is to agree with Jesus' specific and revealed will to "you" about "your specific" situation.

Share a time when God's will for you overshadowed your will and you didn't get what you prayed for.

Have you equated unanswered prayer with being unloved or unseen?

Can you trust Jesus with the outcome, even if you never get the explanation?

Date: _____

Chapter 21: Overcomer

Revelation 12:11 (WEB): They overcame him because of the Lamb's blood, and because of the word of their testimony. They didn't love their life, even to death.

POW! (Pearls of Wisdom): You are an Overcomer, in Christ Jesus!

Share a time when you overcame a tremendous obstacle.

What was your strategy for overcoming?

Author's Info

Chaplain Dorcus Cater, MDIV., BCC, is a board-certified chaplain certified by the Association of Professional Chaplains. She has served as a chaplain in hospice, VA medical centers, the hospital, and as a corporate chaplain for a Fortune 500 Company. She currently serves as an independent chaplain, providing customized spiritual care to individuals, groups, and corporate entities via her company, Boss Chaplain, LLC. She received her Master of Divinity (MDIV) from Mercer University's McAfee School of Theology and her Bachelor of Applied Science (BAS) from Mercer University's College of Continuing and Professional Studies. Her hobbies include storytelling, and refinishing furniture. She is married to Darrell and has one daughter, Althea, and two grandchildren, Elijah and Amelia.

ReShaping Faith Publishing, LLC
4002 Highway 78, Suite 530-213
Snellville, Georgia 30039
reshapingfaith.com
reshapingfaith@yahoo.com

Made in the USA
Columbia, SC
21 May 2025